LIFE SCIENCE

Rattlesnakes:
The Snakes with the Noisy Tails

MICHÈLE DUFRESNE

TABLE OF CONTENTS

Rattlesnake Bites 2
Snake Dens 10
What's for Dinner? 14
Baby Rattlers 16
Glossary/Index 20

PIONEER VALLEY EDUCATIONAL PRESS, INC

RATTLESNAKE BITES

Have you ever seen a rattlesnake? You might have come across one while hiking a rocky trail. Most people would run away if they saw a rattlesnake. That is because a rattlesnake bite can be very dangerous. Their **venom** is extremely strong, but with medical care, a rattlesnake bite is rarely deadly to humans.

Prairie Rattlesnake

Diamondback Rattlesnake

Arizona Ridgenose Rattlesnake

Here is a rattlesnake striking with its fangs extended.

>> There are 32 different species of rattlesnakes. All of them have a triangular head and a rattle on their tails.

Desert Rattlesnake | Speckled Rattlesnake | Twin-Spotted Rattlesnake

Why do rattlesnakes bite? You may be afraid of being bitten by a rattlesnake, but they do not bite unless they are looking for food or protecting themselves.

When they see something dangerous, most rattlesnakes will try to **slither** away without being seen. Others may find a place to hide or stay very still to camouflage themselves with the leaves and ground.

Most of the time, when a rattlesnake bites a person, it is because the person stepped on it by mistake.

When a rattlesnake cannot hide or slither off, it will hiss. Then it will rattle its tail and puff up its body to warn an enemy to back off. The rattle alerts predators to back away, and it protects the snake from being harmed.

When you are walking in heavy brush or rocky areas, look out for rattlesnakes!

Rattlesnakes' tails are covered with hard rings.
These rings are made of **keratin**,
the same thing our fingernails are made of.
As a rattlesnake tightens and loosens
the muscles in its tail,
the segments vibrate against one another,
making a rattling noise.

Rattlesnakes add a new ring to their tail every time they **SHED** their skin.

MORE TO EXPLORE

Rattlesnakes hold their rattles up to protect them as they move around. Sometimes **SEGMENTS** of their tails break off.

Have you ever heard a cat hiss at a dog? Cats do this when they feel threatened. Rattlesnakes also hiss when they feel threatened. Snakes hiss to warn off predators.

MORE TO EXPLORE

Rattlesnakes do not have ears and cannot hear most sounds. They detect movement by sensing **VIBRATIONS** in the ground.

MORE TO EXPLORE

The **WESTERN DIAMONDBACK RATTLESNAKE** is one of the most dangerous rattlesnakes. Its back is covered with dark diamond-shaped patches. Its rattle has a black-and-white pattern like a raccoon's tail. While other rattlesnakes run away from danger, Western Diamondbacks will coil their bodies and raise their heads when threatened.

SNAKE DENS

Rattlesnakes can live in many different **habitats**. Many rattlesnakes live in places with a lot of desert, like the Southwest of the United States. But they can also be found in forests, grasslands, swamps, low bushes, and rocky hills.

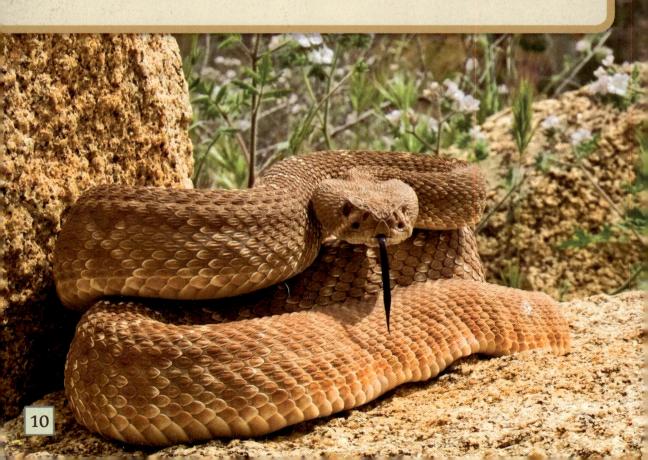

MORE TO EXPLORE

Some rattlesnake families have stayed in the same dens for **OVER 100 YEARS!**

Rattlesnakes live in dens that they make in cracks of rocks. Rattlesnakes often return to the same den year after year, sometimes traveling several miles to get there. Rattlesnakes that live in colder climates **hibernate** in the den for the winter.

Rattlesnakes are cold-blooded. When they get too hot, they head for shade or into a **burrow**. When they get too cold, they find a warm place to rest, like a rock in the sunlight.

When it gets cold outside, you may see snakes lying on the road. The pavement absorbs heat from the sunlight and warms the snakes.

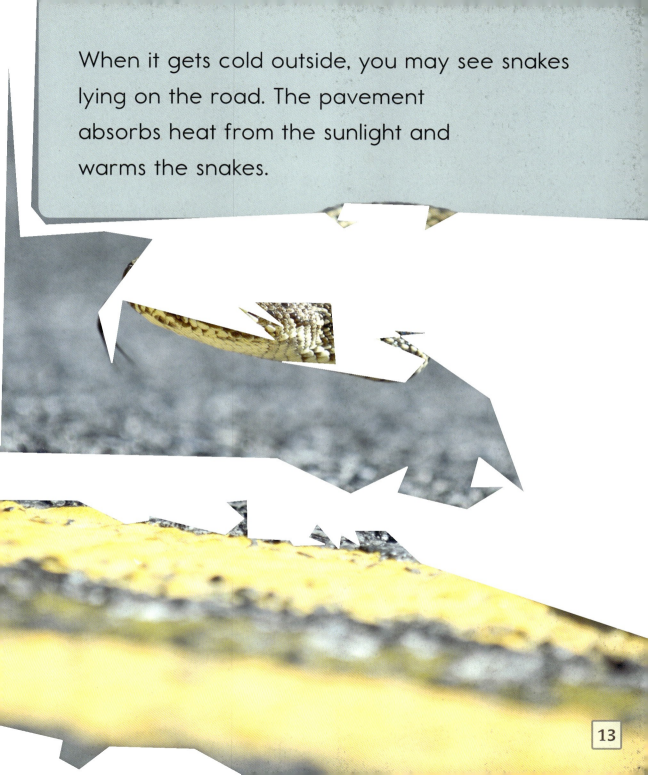

Rattlesnakes are **carnivorous**.
Their favorite foods are small **rodents** and lizards.

They wait quietly until prey comes along and then strike quickly. The venom from their bite makes the prey unable to move.

Rattlesnakes do not have teeth to chew their food, so they have to swallow it whole.

After a rattlesnake swallows its prey, it will hide while the meal is **digested**. This can sometimes take several days and can make the rattlesnake very sleepy. Adult rattlesnakes can survive on just one meal every two weeks.

BABY RATTLERS

Rattlesnake mothers keep their eggs inside their bodies until they hatch. Usually there are eight to ten babies born at one time. The young snakes can quickly find their own food and care for themselves, so the mother will stay with the babies for only a short time. Some mothers will leave as soon as the babies are born.

Newborn rattlesnakes are about ten inches long. At this point, they do not have rattles yet; only a small button on the tips of their tails. But they do have powerful venom and short fangs that make them dangerous. Baby rattlers may strike multiple times if they are disturbed.

Within about 7 to 20 days, the babies shed their skin and grow their first rattle. They will then begin to wander in search of food. Many newborn rattlesnakes do not survive their first year. Some die of hunger, and others are eaten by birds and other animals. Some make it through the summer but then die in the winter if they cannot find a warm den in which to hibernate.

GLOSSARY

burrow
a hole in the ground an animal makes to live in or for safety

carnivorous
an animal that eats meat

digested
breaking down food into a substance that is processed by the body

habitats
places where an animal naturally lives

hibernate
to rest through the winter

keratin
part of the material that makes up hair and nails

rodents
small animals with sharp front teeth

shed
to get rid of something

slither
to move smoothly or quietly

venom
a poison that animals produce to injure or kill other animals

INDEX

bites 2, 4, 14
brush 5
burrow 12
camouflage 4
carnivorous 14
climates 11
cold-blooded 12
dens 10, 11, 18
digested 15
fangs 3, 17
habitats 10
hibernate 11, 18
hiss 5, 8
keratin 6
rattlers 16, 17
segments 6, 7, 19
shed 6, 18, 19
slither 4, 5
Southwest 10
species 3
teeth 14
United States 10
venom 2, 14, 17
vibrations 8
Western Diamondback Rattlesnake 9

Rattlesnakes

Eyes with vertical "cat-like" pupils

Jointed rattle

Triangular head

Scales that are a variety of colors and patterns

Thick bod,

The babies that make it through
the first summer and winter grow rapidly.
Each time they come out of hibernation,
they shed their skin.
Each time they shed their skin,
their rattles grow a new segment.
During the first few years, they may shed
their skin up to three times a year.